EMPLOYED

A guide to connecting churches, corporations, and communities to restore hope and erase and eradicate unemployment!

Written By:

ELDER MARILYN PARKER, EMPLOYMENT CATALYST

Forward By:

Ambassador Ricky D. Floyd – Senior Pastor

Pursuit of God transformation Center

COPYRIGHT PAGE

Sparkman Publishing Company

1425 Purdue

St. Louis, Mo. 63130

ISBN: 9798356428579

Disclaimer

Although the author/publisher has made every effort to ensure that the information in the book was correct at press time and while this publication is designed to provide accurate information in regard to the subject matter covered, the author/publisher assumes no responsibility for errors, inaccuracies, omissions, or any other inconsistencies herein and hereby disclaim any liability to any part for any loss, damage, or disruption caused by errors or omissions, whether such errors or omissions result from negligence, accident, or any other case.

This publication is meant as a source of valuable information for the reader, however it is not meant as a direct substitute for direct expert assistance. If such level of assistance is required, the services of a competent professional should be sought.

Contents

Acknowledgement

I want to thank my late pastor Bishop Arthur L. Kelley, who created an employment servant leader position in community outreach and appointed me for the position.

I want to thank the late Pastor Charles Roach who served with me on my Job Talk radio show, which helped reach out to hundreds and thousands of job seekers. A great motivator, encourager, and mentor, he indeed was to me.

Also, I want to thank my mother, the late Dr. Bessie Reece, my business partner.

Again, I want to thank my husband Mr. Larry Parker, Dr. Dorothy Haire and Elizabeth Brown, Mike Jones, Jackie Dillard, and all my supporters and staff who assisted me greatly through this process.

I also acknowledge and thank each of you for reading this book.

Most of all, I thank Jesus Christ, who counted me faithful and placed me in ministry.

Forward

Fifteen years ago, God allowed me to meet one person that gave me two words that changed the course of our ministry. That lady's name was Marilyn Parker. Those two words were "employment ministry." The Bible tells us that, as the church, we are responsible for feeding the hungry; but the Bible also tells us that if a person doesn't work, they should not eat.

I think the church has done a great job at salvation, a decent job with discipleship, and a wonderful job at feeding people, but a horrible job at assisting people with employment. When Marilyn Parker told me about employment ministry, I immediately wanted to know more. What she described to me was an amazing opportunity to bring hope, healing, and health to communities and meet an immediate need that would impact individuals, families, and communities. It would help decrease crime, increase marriages, make homeownership, and create a great sense of pride within people by having their own.

We dived ten toes deep into this revelation about the ministry of employment that Marilyn Parker gave us, and over the last fifteen years, we have helped over 2,500 people gain employment. This has opened the door for relationships with government officials, which have allowed us to host driver's license restoration, felony expungement, child support reinstatement, voters' registration, etc., and it all started with the insight that Marilyn Parker gave us on employment ministry.

At this very moment, as I write this foreword, we have a Fortune 500 company on our campus offering a $22/hr. job that offers insurance, 401k, college tuition reimbursement, and even transportation from our church to the job site.

For a community where the average individual salary is less than $14,000, this is a game changer. The employment ministry has not only allowed us to tell people that God is good, but it has also allowed them to experience God's goodness.

We have also partnered with another organization, where 16-24 years old who are not in school are unemployed and can get paid training and guaranteed a $20/hr. job after training.

Many times, you hear people say, "We are taking church outside of the walls." Still, the revelation and insight that Marilyn Parker has given us on the importance of employment ministry has not only allowed us to open gates for people but allowed us to tear down walls.

I want to encourage you to look at the ministry and learn from the knowledge released in this book. Be inspired to launch out into the deep. There is a net of fish that needs to be caught, cleaned, cooked, and cast back out to serve as an example. What an amazing opportunity it is to assist people in becoming protectors, providers, and even prophets of the goodness of God.

I want to say "thank you" on behalf of a single mother with four children that came to the ministry unemployed, depressed, and in the process of losing her car and apartment; she was given a 10cent offering by faith. She is now gainfully employed with full-time benefits and is a $500 a month tither now. We helped her get a $15,000/yr. job, then a $30,000/yr. job, and now a $60,000/year job. She is a walking sermon of what God can do.

As a pastor, a businessman, and gatekeeper to the city of Memphis, I want to thank you, Marilyn Parker, for the impact that you have had from over 250miles away.

Ambassador Ricky D. Floyd

Senior Pastor

Pursuit of God Transformation Center.

EMPLOYED

Connecting churches, corporations, and communities to restore hope, erase, and eradicate unemployment!

Introduction

Allow me to introduce myself. My name is Marilyn Parker, and I am an Ordained Evangelist and Employment Catalyst. I have served the church, nonprofit organizations, prisons, and the community at large through workforce development. Serving others in this way brings me great joy and contentment.

I discovered my God-given passion for employment through the church under the leadership of my pastor, the late Bishop Arthur L. Kelley.

I recall decades ago when I found myself among the unemployed. The feeling of being thrust once again into the unemployment line after ten years of a nice work experience led me to devastation, hopelessness, and confusion. The situation was made worst because I didn't know anyone who could assist me in finding another job!

No one in my parents' family who was an adult was unemployed, I felt like I failed everyone important in my life, especially my husband, children, parents, friends, and other family members. I did not have a job anymore! Yes, it was quite a place of trauma for me. I was afraid that my life was going to be different than what I was accustomed to. My deep-seated question became "What shall I do?"

I was very active in my church. I mention church because to me, the church was the place where everyday issues of life were confronted and resolved. I never noticed before that unemployment was never openly discussed or prayed about. We prayed openly and preached about all life issues. "But why not unemployment?" I wondered.

I found myself feeling so ashamed of being unemployed. Every Sunday, I would get up and go to church. I enjoyed our church practice of greeting each other and speaking blessings into each other's lives. But I felt ashamed because of the overbearing secret of being unemployed. They may have been blessed, but I wasn't. All I wanted was someone to mention my problem to, so I could find the help I craved.

Now, don't get me wrong here. At first, I was encouraged by the few people who knew about my circumstance and tried to encourage me. They said, "Keep coming to church." "Do not give up on God." "Just trust in the Lord: He knows exactly when to give you a job." But after a while, all these encouragements but no true help or resources to show for it became disappointing to me. It seemed like many needs were mentioned and addressed throughout the service, all except my need for employment.

The journey to finding a job can be exhausting and debilitating. I can truly say that my God-given passion for helping individuals find employment was sealed inside of me when I finally found employment. The long journey was worth it because I now know that God was developing me to always have compassion for those who are underemployed and unemployed. It is amazing how God works His plan into our lives.

I later accepted my call into the ministry. I was called to be an evangelist. My pastor, Archbishop Arthur L. Kelley, appointed me to be the servant leader in the Community Outreach Department with a focus on employment. I thank God for this appointment!

It allowed me to serve members of our congregation, and soon the unemployed and underemployed throughout communities in other states were employed. Employment became a vital evangelistic tool.

I developed a passion for God's plan for my life. This passion opened doors for me in media, it resulted in making me become the owner of a Christian publication offering job opportunities. This small publication grew into a full-scale magazine named *Sparkman Your Christian Classified Publication.* I later hosted a weekly radio show (The Sparkman Job Talk Show) and a television show (Sparkman2Careers). These two simultaneous shows brought many corporate recruiters and Career Developers right into one's home or car. I also held employment lecture series, seminars, job fairs, and boot camps at churches, community centers, and hotel conference rooms. Later, I had the opportunity to work at one of the leading nonprofit organizations in America that serves the unemployed and underemployed. All these opportunities and experiences equipped and motivated me to become an employment catalyst.

My parents, Mr. Thomas Reece and Dr. Bessie Reece, were both legally blind. Blind individuals can "feel" a room, a person especially. People often say "I feel you," to one another, meaning I completely understand how you are feeling. I am not only listening, but I am also with you. I learned the ability to "feel" from my parents. This additional communication skill is truly a blessing.

My assignment to work on community outreach in the church has taken me from working with churches to working in the community at large, (including prisons) and also working with corporations. Working with and for the unemployed and underemployed has taught me valuable strategies. I would like for you to be enlightened as I unfold how the ministry of employment will also bring social cohesion and moral dimension as it eradicates unemployment and blesses many throughout the land.

I invite you to turn the page, and let's begin.

Chapter 1

Defining

Unemployment and Underemployment

Employment is the position of having work; you might call it labor as well. Perhaps you refer to it as your job, owning your own business or family business, or your own operation where you earn a sustainable living. We not only want employment but sustainable income. This income should be consistent and steady. The income earned provides more than enough to pay bills and purchase food, which makes it a lucrative income. Sustainable income is a level of income from employment we all seek, at the very least. Whether we are employees, self-contractor, or self-employed.

There are three categories of employment status. They are as follows:

1. Workers (self-contractor) are people who perform services but maintain complete control over what will be done, when, and how much will be done. They are in between the employee and self-

employed categories. *Example: Sell your accounting skills to a small business.*

2. Employees are people who work full-time, part-time, or seasonal for an employer and depend upon the employer for specific wages. They work under a contract of employment. *Example: a secretary (full-time), a student dorm monitor (part-time), and a department store sales clerk at Christmas time (seasonal).*

3. Self-employed run their own business and are solely responsible for their success. *Example: freelance writer, cosmetologist, accounting service skills*

When one's definition of employment status has been taken away, and they become unemployed (without a job, voluntary or involuntary) or underemployed (working in a lower capacity than what they are qualified to work in and generally have a job that has lower pay) which may become a dramatic experience. No matter what other issues in life such as sickness, divorce, or grief are; this devastating situation sometimes triumphs over them all. The most important matter in one's life during this time may become the new search to be employed!

We often separate self-employment and/or the business owner from the employment category, but it is still employment. In fact, the government categorizes the business owner as *self-employed.* The measure of devastation may even be greater with the loss of a business. So, measures must be put in place to assist *everyone* in their search for the quality of employment they are seeking.

It is often said we should all own our own businesses. There is a logical pathway. For example, there will always be a need for hospitals and hospital workers; from doctors to housekeepers. Many career field will always have employees, and many of those employees can become self-employed and contract out their abilities and services. Also, at some point, their growth may allow them to become employers and hire employees, paying them sustainable incomes.

An interesting and important fact is that when an individual has been incarcerated, one of the first statuses he/she will have to obtain is employment. Employment is not a law of the land per se, but it is absolutely what we all must obtain to maintain a satisfactory standard of living. Gainfully employed; not unemployed (no job) or underemployed (no sustainable wage).

We all want to see our family, friends, and neighbors become gainfully employed.

I propose that underemployment and unemployment can be eradicated through the intentionality of the church, the local community, and corporations when together they address, teach, and provide resources to those needing these services in all employment statuses. I will explain my proposal as I share the benefits of your church having an employment ministry connecting with community agencies, organizations, and our corporations with the primary focus of restoring hope, erasing and eradicating unemployment.

Chapter 2

The Ministry of Employment in the Church

1Cor, 12:28 says, "And God hath set some in the church, first apostles, secondarily prophets, thirdly teachers, after that miracles, then gifts of healings, **helps**, governments, diversities of tongues."

In accordance with the scripture, the ministry of helps has been set in the church by God. It is an anointed, powerful and vital ministry that is necessary as part of the church structure. It is out of the ministry of helps, that evangelism flourishes throughout our families and communities.

"This Ministry does not operate as a job service, although much information on finding, keeping, and creating jobs is available. This ministry is developed to follow the vision of your church, and all other ministries of help - to fulfill the vision. That one vision that all churches have in common; to reach the loss…that they might be saved.

We have found that building and strengthening unity among the church members through the Ministry of Employment has a positive effect from generation to generation, restoring hope and eradicating Unemployment. This ministry would benefit the church/congregation, the community, and corporations in terms of economic empowerment, social cohesion, and moral dimension. This ministry collaborates with the church, community, and corporation in bringing church members to the status of Employed.

The ministry is defined as helps meaning [1]help according to Merriam Webster

verb \\'help; Southern often 'hep also 'heəp

> *: to do something that makes it easier for someone to do a job, to deal with a problem, etc.: to aid or assist someone*

> *: to make something less severe: to make something more pleasant or easier to deal with*

> *: to give (yourself or another person) food or drink*

Strong's Greek: one who gives help is a helper or servant ...

of one who does what promotes the welfare and prosperity of the church, Colossians 1:25; διάκονοι τοῦ

Chapter 3

Benefits of the Ministry of Employment to the Church.

The Ministry of Employment will benefit the congregation by allowing the church to deal with the one way God defined man would eat. II Thessalonian 3:10 says "For even when we were with you, this we commanded you, that if any would not work, neither should he eat, man must work."

The absence of one's job can be devastating, and as a result of that, many suffer illness and unrest, and soon total hopelessness begins to set in. Often, a person's only concern is employment as they sit in the pew. Sometimes, even the obvious things they should do are not so obvious. The level of shame one may feel keeps them from publicly mentioning this monumental need. The lack of not addressing it from the pulpit helps at some point to make one feel even more ashamed. Identity is so often defined by our titles in the workplace that we become lost when the title is gone.

If one is an active member and giving is a part of what they like to do, but they no longer can give, and they do not know when they will be able to participate in this part of the worship service, it can take a toll on one's mental health. Having this issue addressed in the church gives one a reason to run to the church with expectancy! It allows one to know and realize their value as a person with or without a job and to know that there is always assistance for whatever you need. You do not have to tackle this alone. The ministry having people and resources to assist you and connect you to community agencies that will connect you to the right corporations for gainful employment or SBA administrators will be invaluable if they are unable to do this.

The Ministry of Employment has Five Key benefits:

1. Sustainable Income for All church members= Economic Empowerment.
2. Unity and Growth Within the Church.
3. Social Cohesion.
4. Moral Dimension.
5. Corporate Involvement.

Chapter 4

Sustainable Income for All church members

The goal of the Ministry of Employment is to see that everyone is cared for and getting their needs met. That economically and spiritually, things are well, and if not, there is a space where this can be worked on and attained. The Ministry of Employment comes into full force from within the congregation. Members of the congregation serve in this ministry. There is a team leader and four other servants leading this ministry.

This ministry will begin with offering help to all those in the congregation who seek help in their employment status. Whether the need is employment or entrepreneurship, help would now be available. Let us keep in mind that when there is a lack, professional aptitude does not matter. From the business owner to the one with a G.E.D, to one released from prison to with a Ph.D., everyone who needs job search assistance or income creation can receive help from this ministry.

All that is required of them is that they are willing and ready to be accountable for themselves, and we know they are. This ministry teaches one how to fish and not simply give them the fish. Not only will members have the employment status they seek, but they also will earn a sustainable income. (A sustainable income allows one to meet their needs now and, in the future).

There will also be an increase in tithes and offerings. Many members have a desire to give in the offering. Some even feel guilty when they cannot participate in this part of the worship service. Yes, some members became homeless because of unemployment and underemployment. Some of these situations may leave an individual without any income. If their circumstances remain the same, they may feel so bad that they decide to discontinue fellowship with others until their situation changes.

Sustainable income is a must and not optional. It should neither be considered for one to work and also able to pay bills. It must be an intentional goal to achieve sustainable income.

One needs to be planted while in their search and surrounded by the people and resources they need to attain this goal. The Ministry of Employment will connect the individual to both, allowing them the emotional support and tools needed to fulfill the desire for sustainable income.

Next, sustainable income becomes the goal of the family. This ministry leads one to build generational wealth. There will be many to surpass sustainable income with wealth creation, but it will all begin with resources in place that can be found in the Ministry of Employment. We all have gifts. Many of these gifts will bring entrepreneurs who will become employers. There are treasures in the church that will be exposed through the ministry of employment. Over time, this will bring economic empowerment throughout society.

Chapter 5

Unity and Growth Within the Church

There is no difference in how one feels as one stands and sings the praise and worship songs or participates in hymn singing when one has a great need in their home. Maybe one has a cell phone cut off, another has a late payment notice on the car note, one has a child in college and tuition is due, mortgage or rent. Perhaps a gentleman has just been released from prison after serving many years and came to church seeking hope in this situation. All parties feel the same. The lack from all these situations smells, feels, and creates the same hopeless energy!

There is often a great division in economic status even in the church. We separate even in our seating in the church. Some may feel others are holier or more anointed according to where they sit. Some are just not comfortable up front. All the young people may sit together. Perhaps your Amen group and rowdy praises are in the back of the church. There are all kinds of reasons why we separate, even in the church. But just as in all things, when we come together with the same mission and sometimes the same concern, we find unity. We often have picnics and potlucks which are wonderful ways to fellowship. Sometimes, those with an employment need will not come out to the picnic or the potluck dinner. The need for an income has taken much of their thoughts of relaxing, so they miss out. The ministry of employment assures them they belong at the festivities by restoring hope, along with resources. The bond that will be formed and unity that will spread throughout our buildings will be contagious and will only multiply members.

All members are now boasting of their church's obligation to their members and guests. Everyone can now participate in bringing a guest to church! The members share The Employment ministry offers hope by helping to place members into resources that will lead to gainful employment. After gainful employment, there is economic empowerment for all congregation members.

Members in the congregation who are part of the ministry of employment have a feeling of belonging and not embarrassment. Members in the congregation who are now in their job search tend to also feel belonging and not embarrassed. Through this ministry, the congregation is helping in fulfilling their moral dimension. We are concerned about our neighbor's quality of life, and this ministry demonstrates that to the maximum. The unity will continue to grow stronger and stronger.

In the church, engagement lies a driving force. The employment ministry is a great engaging ministry for your church. Serving all people with the opportunities they deserve in the workforce! This ministry forces the church to build relationships within the community they are in, which is a total win-win situation!

We are our brother's Keeper.

Chapter 6

Social Cohesion

We have social cohesion forming amongst members, regardless of age, color, gender, or wealth status in a great way. As we learn to openly share without embarrassment our need for sustainable income and find the help, we need, to openly encourage one another, the in this way, this ministry set-up will cause your church to grow expeditiously.

The ministry builds relationships with our community resources, also known as "wraparound services" within the community. These services are offered through many of our nonprofit's organizations. Wraparound services are what this team masters. One of the ministry leaders will have the special assignment of having knowledge and partnership within the community organizations to refer and follow the individual in their employment search and provide support from within the church's walls. Employment Services (resume writing, mock interviewing, dress for success, conflict resolution) are found within the community with our nonprofit organizations at no charge who, thus, connect with our corporations and businesses for employment. Those seeking small business assistance can also acquire the needed information. This relationship between the church and community organizations promises to render great results through its strategic efforts and planning that are already established.

These community services are often not known to families in the community. We all know that our nonprofit agencies understand the major benefits and success of having wrap-around services to support our community. Now the church will build relationships to establish this successful model for the Ministry of Employment. This ministry connects the community in such a great way. It's a win-win for the church, community agencies, and corporations. Social cohesion will restore hope, put millions to work and in business and help eradicate the unemployment and underemployment epidemic.

Chapter 7

Moral Dimension

Moral dimension is a part of "love thy neighbor as thyself." It shows we care for one another's quality of life. When we do not just hand our brothers/sisters a job or business opportunity but connect with them. Addressing the possibility of a need shows care and is felt. Moral dimension expresses Empathy.

Empathy is a strong component of the moral dimension; it is demonstrated by one having the ability to understand and recognize how another is feeling. The ministry of employment takes a   step forward by providing services to the member/visitor that will help to sustain families from generation to generation.

Through this ministry, the congregation is helping in fulfilling their moral dimension. Through the efforts and work of the Ministry of Employment within the church, connecting with the community organizations, agencies, and corporations provides opportunities for sustainability.

The impact on the community is strongly affected by these members going back to their neighborhoods and families, bringing more people to their church. The excitement is electrifying. Being a part of such a worship experience offers such hope to the people. To place members into a position that will lead to gainful employment, which in turn brings economic empowerment to your entire city, restoring hope, erasing and eradicating underemployment and unemployment.

CHAPTER 8

CORPORATE INVOLVEMENT

Poverty is a concern worldwide, and tackling this problem is what the Ministry of employment strategically needs to do. No group, organization, institute, nor corporation will be able to successfully do this. It will take the church, community, and Corporations. All hands must be on deck!

The benefits are too many to number for corporations; listing a few:

   a) Corporations can build a reputation for being active and contributing members of the community.
   b) Corporations build trust as they forge alliances with community agencies and small businesses.
   c) Employment issues such as retention can go down tremendously.
   d) Open positions can be filled more swiftly.
   e) They, too, can all become volunteers more easily within the community.

Collectively all benefit greatly from the involvement of the Corporations. Lastly, this allows corporations to be involved not only as employers but also as supporters!

Chapter 9

The Prison Ministry and Retention in the Workplace

Finally, the ministry of employment will help greatly with your prison ministry and retention in the workforce.

Even if a church does not have a prison ministry but has members with their family members in prison. That family member can now assist in helping their relative. One of the many challenges he/she will face is obtaining gainful employment. It is most important that "gainful employment" is available.

There are great jobs and career opportunities for those returning home from prison. Now, the ministry of employment is serving the community in an even greater way. Families are growing in the church. Recidivism (men/women returning to prison) is decreasing, and crime rates are reduced.

Social cohesion and moral dimension fuel one's hope! Hope is spreading through the ministry as it travels from church, community, and corporations.

Employers have huge retention problems. Many of the components shared within the ministry of employment will help profoundly. The retention problems add considerably to our countries' unemployment and underemployment rate.

I am honored and excited to work with you and look forward to us building our churches, communities, and corporations together. I am available for all your questions or concerns and can be reached via email at

Eldermarilynparker@theministryofemployment.org

Train the Trainer
A Strategic Part of the Employment Ministry

Train the Trainer is exclusively designed to assist any willing church or ministry with a desire to help their members and visitors with sustainable income and more!

Who should attend this powerful information pack training?

YOU (pastors, volunteers, human resource professionals, community leaders).

Get consultations on how to formulate an employment plan for your congregation

Get support from others who have successfully started to like the programs

Leave having met others who support the ministry of employment mission.

Learn about customizing your church's employment ministry

Learn how to partner with nonprofit government agencies, educational institutions, and corporations

Learn how to start this ministry NOW email: eldermarilynparker59@gmail.com

Marilyn Parker/Employment Catalyst/314-651-1880

Endorsements

I am delighted by this fantastic piece of literature that has indeed emphasized the simplicity and relevance of a strategized ministry of employment in every sector of society, including churches, communities, and nonprofit organizations or corporations. This ministry tends to positively address the hopelessness and devastation of an unemployed or underemployed individual who is also an unhappy human. Also, we get to see some of these benefits that come with creating this vital sector called the ministry of employment in the church and society as a whole. This fosters sustainable income for all church members who are also members of the society, promotes unity, growth in the church, societal enhancement, social cohesion, moral dimension, and a great deal of corporate involvement. The author's ability to capture the beauty of development, unity, hope, happiness, and purpose as the result of a fruitful ministry of employment. Whether in church or the society at large, as seen in each of the chapters, left me encouraged and enlightened, and I consider this an absolute skill of expressive writing. Each paragraph carefully and concisely brought me into a position to better appreciate the key benefits required for a progressive and developed church, community, corporation, or society facing the problem of unemployment or underemployment by providing various alternative means towards eradicating such problems and that simply gave a room for a great deal of enlightenment. I am encouraged by the author's skill and expertise, and in awe of the wonders, this book entails. You are a prolific writer endowed with clarity in writing.

Doris Foster/ Nigeria

Marilyn Parker is the ultimate advocate for the employed and unemployed people in the church. In the book, "Employed", Marilyn Parker wakes up leaders to help those with jobs and no jobs, and those that are stuck in a dead-end job. If you are looking to change careers and make a difference, I highly recommend this book. "Employed" is a game-changer!

Dr. Robert Watkins/ Conqueror Worldwide/
Windermere, FL 34786

Endorsements

Marilyn has the unique skill set of inspiring clients, while providing the goal of getting people hired. I have been blessed to hear her passion in several ways. She has shared her passion of Faith Based Workforce development through her radio, TV and print media. Always consistent in her quest of getting those less fortunate employed. I've witnessed her ability to work with ex-felons who many have given up on. Marilyn uses her understanding of their plight coupled with successful examples that concludes in positive results. Her acumen of time management and people management are above par. She orchestrates many in galvanizing the troops. This skill set denotes community impact that few can say they have. Any organization that can be blessed with Marilyn Parker's talent, will benefit from an economic and social impact perspective.

Dr. Lance E. McCarthy/Ferguson 1000/St. Louis, Mo.

My professional relationship with Ms. Parker spans 15 years. As the director of the Missouri State Highway Patrol Recruiting Division.

Ms. Parker coordinated multiple recruiting events in which we endeavored to mentor and establish employment opportunities for offenders and those in underserved communities. Ms. Parker conducted radio programs, marketing, and face to face meetings that played a crucial role in making these endeavors successful.

The most prominent, and important attribute I have observed over the years regarding Ms. Parker and her approach to workforce development, is her outstanding ability to communicate. Ms. Parker is a well-established, organized, motivated and reliable advocate for workforce development, and community resources for offenders and others. I have observed her tireless dedication.

I believe Ms. Parker has provided a must-read guide with a clear framework

"Employed"

A guide to connect churches, corporations, and communities to erase and eradicate unemployment and restore hope!

People will be reading this guide and profiting from it for a very long time.

Roger Whittler, Capt. Retired/ /St. Louis, Mo.

The End

Made in the USA
Middletown, DE
18 October 2022

12977563R00024